We are being painted
into nature's blue silence,
quite unaware that we are
... the artists.

~ Candice James

(excerpt from poem 'Blue Silence')

Also by Candice James

Short Shots 2 *(Silver Bow Publishing)* 2023
Spiritual Whispers *(Silver Bow Publishing)* 2023
Imagination's Reverie *(Silver Bow Publishing)* 2023
Atmospheres *(Silver Bow Publishing)* 2023
The Depth of the Dance *(Silver Bow Publishing)* 2023
Behind the One-Way Mirror *(Silver Bow Publishing)* 2022
The Call of the Crow *(Silver Bow Publishing)* 2021
he Path of Loneliness *(Inanna Publications)* 2020
Rithimus Aeternam *(Silver Bow Publishing)* 2019
Haiku Paintings *(Silver Bow Publishing)* 2019
The 13th Cusp *(Silver Bow Publishing)* 2018
Fhaze-ing *(Silver Bow Publishing)* 2018
The Water Poems *(Ekstasis Editions)* 2017
Short Shots *(Silver Bow Publishing)* 2016
City of Dreams *(Silver Bow Publishing)* 2016
Merging Dimensions *(Ekstasis Editions)* 2015
Colors of India *(Xpress Publications India)* 2015
Purple Haze *(Libros Libertad)* 2014
A Silence of Echoes *(Silver Bow Publishing)* 2014
Shorelines *(Silver Bow Publishing)* 2013
Ekphrasticism *(Silver Bow Publishing)* 2013
Midnight Embers *(Libros Libertad)* 2012
Bridges and Clouds *(Silver Bow Publishing)* 2011
Inner Heart, a Journey *(Silver Bow Publishing)* 2010
A Split in the Water *(Fiddlehead Poetry Books)* 1979

Blue Silence

by

Candice James

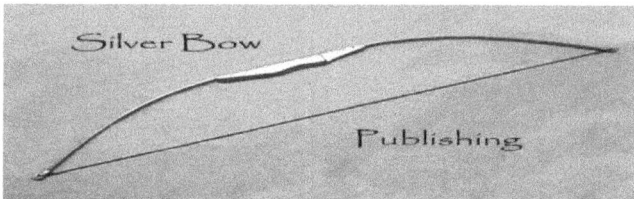

Silver Bow Publishing

Box 5 – 720 – 6th Street,
New Westminster, BC
V3C 3C5   CANADA

Title: Blue Silence
Author: Candice James
Copyright © 2024 Silver Bow Publishing
Cover Painting: "Blue Waters" painting by Candice James
Layout/Design: Candice James
ISBN: 9781774033012 (print)
ISBN: 9781774033029 (ebk)j

Library and Archives Canada Cataloguing in Publication

Title: Blue silence / by Candice James.
Names: James, Candice, 1948- author.
Identifiers: Canadiana (print) 20240330773 | Canadiana (ebook)
2024033082X | ISBN 9781774033012
   (softcover) | ISBN 9781774033029 (Kindle)
Subjects: LCGFT: Poetry.
Classification: LCC PS8569.A429 B58 2024 | DDC C811/.54—
dc23

For God,
in reverence of all his creations.

Blue Silence

Contents

Blue Silence

Conversations Of The Trees

The atmosphere thickens.
    The sky darkens
        as the stately Firs stretch
    and scribble an "S.O.S." on the air
        we can't see with the naked eye.

Beneath the grass and soil,
    the underground root system
        sends steady communications:
north, east, west, south. "N.E.W.S."
        with up to the minute reports
of the threatening surface storm.

We pay no attention
    to this intellectual social vegetation.
        These keepers of the oxygen balance.
    These stalwart sentinels of Earth's eco-systems.

We never stop to imagine
a world without trees.
        A world without oxygen.
            A world without human life.

The atmosphere is thin. The darkness pales.
    The stately Firs relax. The S.O.S. cancelled.
        We just continue walking
    oblivious to the conversations of the trees.

A Deadly Splash Of Green

There is dust on the sidewalk
Rust on the leaves
And a forest alive with a deadly splash of green

I sit in a separate space
Beneath a dappled blue sky
Content in my makeshift tent

I am a wayward poplar
Surrounded by evergreens;
A cedar growing roses
On a desert dune of melting snow

In the corner of my eye I see a random tear
Dropping from a weeping willow's aching heart
In the edge of my ear I hear a whisper
Beckoning me deeper into the forest

I start to crumble, like the ancient relic I am,
Into the dust on the sidewalk,
The rust on the leaves
Exhaling my final breath
In a deadly splash of green

A Season That Never Dies

The autumn leaves drift and float down
        whispering to the river
as they kiss the songs of the dying season
           onto the lips of her tear-stained face.

This is the pale blue mirror of sky
           and the glimmer and glimpse
      of the living paintings
         moving and swaying
    beyond the shadow of the veil.

Inside this dream I am
      there is an echo of beautiful music
        calling me home and home
           again and again.

Just like the autumn leaves drifting down
      soon I'll drift onto the pale blue mirror
        to reside with the living paintings,
        moving and swaying
      beyond the shadow of the veil
        to the songs of a season
          that never dies.

A Small Destruction

We sat, as usual,
Chilled by the late September wind,
Huddled to our coffee cups,
Haloed by our cigarette smoke.

Just yesterday
We had commented on that tree:
How beautiful,
As it began changing costume
In the hush of Autumn's breath;
Stately, regal;
And somehow,
We considered it a friend.

We sat,
Witnessing its mutilation
And ultimate murder
At the harsh hands
Of two scruffy men in a city truck.

A haunting sorrow crept over us,
Indescribable,
Tugging at the corners of our eyes.

We sat in silence
Amidst the noise of annihilation
Inside this small destruction.

We left early.
Words had been destroyed too.

A Small Winter Sky

A small winter sky
       turned white with snow
              dresses the trees in sparse white robes
              emulating a gathering of fallen angels
       praying to the small winter sky
       for a redemption of sorts.

There is a feeling of inclusion
       beneath a small winter sky
              that becomes lost
                     under a vast sky.

Small towns,
       small sky
              less people
                     more communication
                     more empathy

Yes,
       there is definitely
              something very special
              and very warm
                     for those that
              live and breathe
              beneath a small winter sky.

A Smooth White Rabbit

I see the colours reverse through themselves.
The moon turns inside out.
The sun burns into ebony embers
and spirals and spins in the palm of my hand.

This is a stir of coloured edges,
A field of slim fashion designer canes and walking sticks,
and beneath the overhang of swaying petals
a smooth white rabbit
conjures up invisible magicians of light
to harvest the flowers' most precious dreams.

There are quantum worlds within the flowers:
Sub-atomic melodies and miniature dancers
moving to the beat of a different drummer
in a different dimension
of unknown reasons and seasons.
Glass slippers, Cinderellas and Prince Charmings.

In the lush velvet underbelly
Of this pastel tranquility
Wishes are granted and dreams come true.
Opaque plates of glass slide over each other
And etch their image and essence
Onto the pale-yellow feathered ceiling
Of waxed jazz recordings.

In the solace of a crimson heartbeat,
A smooth white rabbit
Pushes the shiny gold button,
Unzips the pristine dream
And the music plays.

A Spring Too Far

Wandering through this place I should know,
        the once familiar signposts
    dotting the now treacherous landscape
          have become blurred
     and unreadable
     in the fogged climate
         that continuously invades
           my days and nights.

The summer winds have faded.
     The autumn leaves have fallen.
       The chill of winter
       is too cold this year
         to hold any promise
         of spring or renewal.

    Wandering around,
       lost in this place I should know
         but don't recognize,
      I stand in silent hope
     wishing for,
   and dreaming of,
Spring is too far.

A Stir Of Moonbeams

I feel a stir of moonbeams at the start
and then the glow of stars light up my heart.
I hear a mix of echoes drawing near
and what was once a whisper now rings clear.

The colours are now brighter than before.
The yellow broom bush just outside my door
accentuates the scented lilac rose.
Each blade of grass vibrates in soft repose.

The atmosphere's alive with sweet birdsong.
I recognize the tune and hum along.
I see a sunrise lighting up the sea
and raindrops on my cheek are kissing me
and all the while, all the while I'm missing thee.

The stir of moonbeams slows and then dissolves
The edge of night unzips and then evolves.
An old familiar voice is calling me
singing soft a haunting melody.

I hear a mix of echoes in my mind
inside this firmament that God designed.
I feel a stir of moonbeams in my soul
that turns my weary, aching heart to gold.

I feel the touch of God's hand at the end
I'll never break again ... now I can bend,

A Touch Of Winter

I stand inside a stark white silence.
A film noire reverses
in opaque ghostly images
and rolls in a backlit sequence
of yesterday's song and dance.

Muted memories eddy and whirl.
The white silence is deafeaning.

A rundown wooden bridge
creaks, heaves, and moans
under the weight
of each new snowfall.

Swelling and shrinking
it flexes weaker each year
toward its long time companions,
the barren trees that stand rigid,
inside the invisible freeze frames
on december's cutting room floor.

I walk inside this winter loneliness,
toward the distant mountains,
alone with only the echoes of my mind.

I move
into the mist
and blend with the sky.

I walk
through this touch of winter
untouched.

Acanthus Mollis

Native floral headdress,
showy feathers bright,
reminiscent of a neon rainbow.

Scented dancers swaying,
marching to the beat of nature's drum
in an other-worldly distant thrum.

Seeds of cosmic dust
bedding down in earthly terrain;
gold born of rust
and teeming acid rain,
floated to this new domain
disguised itself to feign
resemblance to surrounding seeds
burrowing between the weeds.

A masquerading petal faces
obliterating alien trace
now, donning native dress
to cover nakedness.

A fish with faded fin,
unnoticed it fits in.

Afternoon Shadows

Late afternoon shadows fall soft on the street.
A gentle wind nuzzles the trees.
I close my eyes and listen to my breath
trying to identify that momentary stillness
cleft in between the in between.

I'm adrift in a sea of dominoes
on a checkerboard ocean of half-played lives
       and second hand gestimate sighs.

And there ... at the edge of my vision
I'm suddenly aware of approaching ghosts.
       Some know my name
       and some are strangers.

I walk with uncertainty's wisdom
between battered pillars and burning posts
       feeling the flame
       aware of the dangers,

And now the afternoon shadows have blended.
The light of the day is almost ended.
The sun's bent down on its knees.
as twilight enters with eloquent ease.

I close my eyes and listen to my breath
as dusk wanders slowly away from day's death.

All The Colours Bleed Into One
(Ekphrastic poem to painting by Janet Kvammen)

Flowers, in the attic spun,
watch twilight drip through blue.
When all the colours bleed into one
the truth comes shining through.

Beneath the brilliant flowers, pale images emerge:
I see a world within a world -- my pulse begins to surge.
This world of mystery beneath the orange and yellow
echoes ancient history in whispers soft and mellow.

> *As it is above*
> *so it is below.*
> *It's just a different version*
> *of what we see and know.,*

Through eternal hours the flowers feed the earth;
and the roots feed the flowers, from death to rebirth.

As purple twilight ebbs and flows
patches of blue rest in repose
then all the colours bleed into one;
beneath a sleeping sun.

All The While

Mellowed in muted fascination,
swaying in shades of exultation,
leaves fall from trees like crepe paper and wool
in the afterglow of nature's pull.
Reflecting through this gentle shine
water's repast turned to wine.
As Chardonnay flows through the mind
Light spools and pools and then unwinds.

       And all the while the shoreline listens.
       And all the while the ocean glistens.

Perchance an eagle's flying by.
Perhaps a tear falls from his eye.
As Autumn leaves now undress
and wait for fall to confess
she's fallen prey to winter's charms
embraced inside his icy arms.

       And all the while the shoreline listens.
       And all the while the ocean glistens.

The sands fall in the hourglass.
I slowly watch the moments pass.
I lay with ear pressed to the ground
in silence listening for the sound
of footsteps whispering your return
and once again love's flame will burn

       And all the while the shoreline listens.
       And all the while the ocean glistens.

Antique Harbour

The golden grift of sea shade,
speckled with shimmering pastels.
Reflections of a landscape on the wing,
dipping, brush-like,
into the chameleon waters of the bay.

A stained-glass antique harbour
of broken shiplap and dulled hardwood;
peeling paint and barnacled hulls
decorate the boats that have fallen ill
in the jaws of disrepair.

This is the way of the old men and the sea:
Lackluster fishermen.
Past their prime.
Past the point of no return.
Living out their salty days
on the tears of an ebbing tide.

Once there were tall ships.
Gleaming fishing vessels.
Muscular young men
with a fever in their soul
and their hearts set like a sail.

Once there were younger days:
Glistening boats.
Gleaming hulls,
and too many fish to catch.

Once upon a time,
        long ago,
    this harbour was alive.

Autumnal Equinox

I looked up from my papers
and suddenly it was winter.
the trees across the street hung with snow;
and all the flowers dead and gone.

The frost-split pavement
was ablaze in the cut of a January sun.

I tried to shake off the chill of the season
as its icy hands squeezed my soul.

I moved to the beat of a slow minuet
playing in three-quarter time

A million moments passed me by.
I turned back to my papers ...
        and then ...
when I looked up again,
suddenly it was summer
and spring was only a passing thought
in the autumnal equinox of my mind.

Crimson Watering Can

There stands
the crimson watering can:

paint stretched
and peeling

under a blistering
July sun

beside the white
begonias.

Diamond Day

I dreamed a sparkling azure sky
        draped loosely
above an ocean of sparkling diamonds.

The diamonds prismed into rainbows
and shone for a moment in eternity.

Then there was a silvering
        to the sky.
   It flickered against
the disappearing rainbows.

Then the diamond day
slid through twilight's fingers
into the dark purple palm of dusk.

Dragonfly Dance

Dragonfly,
　　　　with long sleek body,
　　delicately perched on a green stem of life,
　　　　　　then careening upward:
　　　　riding a sunbeam, kissing the sky,
rippling the tranquility of dampened rainbow strings,
　　　　coaxing the music within... without,
scoring new harmonies into nature's symmetry,
　　　　　　gliding through glades,
　　　　　　sliding on currents,
　　swimming through the atmosphere
whispering secrets to the rain.

Dragonfly:
　　　　diva of dance,
　　　　　　　ballerina of beauty,
balancing on the tip of god's paintbrush,
　　　　accenting nature's masterpiece
　　　　　　　with your graceful dance.

　　　Dance dragonfly ...
　　　　　　　dance.

Melodies And Scents

A table sits in quiet repose
at the edge of the silent room.
On it, an antique speaker with no frame
and a vase alive with dead flowers.

Doors open and close
as I approach and pass through them.

As I move through many unfamiliar rooms
I think of the antique speaker with no frame
and I wonder at the songs played through it;
and I wonder if the dead flowers in the vase
were roses or carnations or wildflowers.

Melodies and scents
are such a big part of life
        and when they're gone, they're gone;
        so take time to enjoy the songs
            and smell the flowers
                    as you pass by.

Midnight Blue

Early evening dusk
blankets the fog and mist
in a watery kiss
perched on the rain's dropped lips.

Driving through a corridor of trees
a soft focus of twilight glow
peppers the entrance for impending night.

The soft mellow intonations
of long-ago sonatas
caress the passing moments
bleeding midnight blue
through the fading dusk.

North Of Skagway

North of Skagway
the water sparkles,
      crisper
than a morning dawn breaking;

and the snow glistens
      softer
than a white velvet rose.

Just north of Skagway
   I stand alone
at the ship's guard rail
   in total awe
 of nature's beauty
and God's noble design.

Early Morning Haunting

Through the foggy lens
of an early morning haunting
the ghosts of summer,
windblown voices
and hazy dreams
    still linger
in the blue shadows
  of a dying star

A pearl scarf of frost glistens
under a red rising Sun.
A lone gull cries to the wind
leaving its imprint
in the thick atmosphere
of a muted October sky.

My footsteps crunch and crackle
on a scatter of pebbles and leaves
that whisper secrets
into the outstretched palms
of this early morning haunting.

      I watch the sun rise;
      ash to ember to flame.
      I listen to the wind;
      silence to whispers to voices.

I'm alone, but not alone.
I walk with ghosts
in the blue shadows
of this early morning haunting ...
      haunted.

The Cedars

Deep within the quiet park land glade
I chanced to hear a poet softly speaking.
in words so strange and yet so eloquent
beneath a sky of lonely cedars creaking.

And I was drawn into the surreal glow
of poetry's majestic flowing sound;
the speaker shone upon a make-shift stage
and stood atop a sparkling grassy mound.

I stood stock-still and fully hypnotized
caught up inside that magical greenbelt.
Each gesture and each word that poet spoke
described so perfectly the way I felt.

Then ... morning broke on sharpened spokes of sun;
the dream unraveled, and it came undone.

But some nights, still, I hear that poet speaking
and swear I hear a lonely cedar creaking.

The Small Barnacled Rocks Of Yesterday

Lately at the edge of night
on the precipice of fading consciousness
the past creeps into my impending sleep
      on little cat feet.

I am a small child again,
laying in my training bed
at the Crescent Beach cottage,
listening to the lapping of the waves
as they kiss the twilit shoreline.

An absolute peace and contentment
wash over me as I lie in my happiness
   listening to the ocean's sighs
     falling softly into dreams
        of sandbars,
         seaweed,
        tidal pools
and small barnacled rocks;
where tomorrow I will build castles,
    wade the tidal pools
      and search
  for tiny crabs and starfish
under the small barnacled rocks
  of my long-lost yesterdays.

Blue Silence

In this slow grooved moment
of powder blue silence,
the glide of nature's paintbrush
and the whisper of the wind
are the only sounds we hear.

At the water's edge
a cold damp creeps into our feet,
winding itself up our legs
like an icy vine.

We rub our hands together
thinking it may warm our legs
and hold the numbness at bay,
but the numbness continues to climb.

We begin a slow jog around the lake.
Fogged breath, blowing back in our face,
peppers the chilled air
making it bearable,
almost welcome.

As we jog
the lake whispers secrets to us;
and the wind blushes our cheeks
a rosier shade of red.

We are being painted
into nature's blue silence,
quite unaware that we are ...
                              the artists.

The Flowers Nod

The flowers nod in the wind
as the prairie chinook manifests its presence
and the leaves seem to sizzle in its wake.

Violets and wildflowers adorn the broom bushes
and sway in the fields of tall grasses and wheat.

Yellow, purple, red, green, and pink
mixed in amongst the white
and nestled in the palm of God
and nature's afternoon rhapsody.

The sun and the sky hold court
accentuating nature's grand domain
and the flowers nod in acknowledgment
to this bold colourful statement
spilled from the master's bush,
        confirming
the grandeur of God's firmament.

Mini Dunes

A little further out west
on the eastern edge
of a rising wet moon,
teardrops begin to form and fall
onto a dry crusted beach.

The sand has long since coalesced
into mini dunes of pale grey and charcoal
a checkerboard sequence scene
    dotting a seaside
enclosing a hidden once upon a time
    long ago beach.

       Now,
     crumbles,
into broken images
of yesterday's dreams.
These mini dunes whisper
of their glory days;
of glittering sunsets
and crystal blue waters
and summer crowds
laughing and kissing
the days alive again
on these mini dunes
of long, long ago.

Inner Forests

Down the soft mossy trails
    that line the inner forests of mind
        there are hidden beaches
    with sand sprayed gazebos standing tall
        amidst fractured rock and shells.
The glitter of amber and shimmer of abalone
    twinkle and shine in the glint
        of a high noon sun.

The haunting song of a lone violin
    echoes in the strum of my soul
        and on the strings of my heart.

    My breathing
        comes measured and slow
            in the calm of the fading
            afternoon glow.

The tide's coming full
    in the push of moon's pull
        encroaching on the horizon.

    The soft mossy trails and lazy beaches
        that line the inner forests of my mind,
    melt into the edge of daylight's ebb
        and dissolve inside night's top hat
            on the brim of an ebony sky.

Dust Scatters

A black satin scarf
      floats
  in a clear summer sky
dark as an oil slick on water.

Newborn stars polish the satin.

Silence rises up;
      a mountain permeating
      the story the stars are telling.

Wind picks up,
      turns the pages;
      dust scatters.

Rain At The Ready

An image in the distance
        edges closer
with seemingly uncertain steps

        sleepwalking,
            yet semi-awake

rain at the ready
yet hesitant to fall

        awaiting
    the wind's command

What Are The Birds Inferring?

Today is one of those odd days
that seem to have no meaning
until something unusual happens.

I sit in my car waiting; watching.
A group of thirty-plus starlings swoop onto
the seemingly dead lawn on my right.
They dig at the soil and weeds, scatter around.

      A second group of birds arrives
and starts to dig a few feet away from group one.

The sound of a car begins to approach.
The birds scatter onto two separate rooftops
      keeping to their own *'clan'*.

A couple of minutes pass then ...
group one swoops down onto another dead lawn
on my left ... then a minute later
the second group swoops down
and pecks and saunters
a few feet away from group one.

      They don't mix.

Could this be Avian discrimination?
Or possibly even... Avian racism?

Or just a matter of common courtesy.

At Rest In The Color Of Lilac

I'm at rest in the color of lilac
      as I walk through a timeless garden
          of damp iris and blue Christmas rose
      awash in the fading days of long, long ago.

      There's an old gray-haired grandmother
          setting the table for her absentee son
          and lesser-known granddaughter.

      There's a well-kept backyard
          and a pale green canvas swing
               creaking and swaying
                  in time with the wind
          and a synchronized finger-painting scene.

      She stands at the window
          awaiting the arrival of her dinner guests
               that never will arrive.

Sometimes I glimpse her harsh cruel eyes
      that disguise the weave of her tender heart,
          but only when I'm at rest
               in the pastel color of lilac
          walking the timeless garden
    of damp iris and blue Christmas rose
          awash in the color and scent of lilac
          and the fading twilight
               of long, long ago.

A Fresh Violet

The sweaters are empty now.
Closets are overflowing.

We were winter people,
        violets growing in the snow.

                Winged angels of death.
                Masked robbers of breath.

        Lovers unconsummated for so long.

        I'll give you a fresh violet
                surrounded by snow.

                Breathe on it ...
                        that it may live forever.

This Tree
(a sonnet)

(As a child I played in Queen's Park New Westminster, BC and still today I love to visit this beautiful park and sit under that same old tree I've sat under through childhood's page, middle age and the golden years)

In silence stands a tree that's always been.
With love's initials carved into her bark;
In seasonal and changing shades of green
The fingerprints of time have left their mark.
She's home to Robins, Wrens and Stellar Jays
And lovers lost in languished sweet embrace.
In childhood, teenage days and adult plays
She's witnessed smiles and tears upon my face.
I've watched her dance in every season's arm;
In nakedness and wrapped in shiny leaves.
And as she swoons, falls prey to Autumn's charms
I've watched the dying leaves fall from her sleeves.

A sentinel, this tree has always been.
She still stands tall and oh, the sights she's seen!

A River Flows
(a villanelle)

A river flows beneath the breeze
upon a broken stony bed
adorning rock hewn shore and trees.

An eagle eye peers down and sees
a silver salmon bobbing head.
A river flows beneath the breeze.

The droning buzz of swarming bees
outside a rusty run-down shed.
Adorning rock hewn shore and trees.

Loosened now from winter's freeze,
arisen springing from the dead,
a river flows beneath the breeze.

A splash of crocus clings with ease
to newborn soil rich and red
adorning rock hewn shore and trees.

The mountains bend down on their knees.
The sunset bows its weary head.
A river flows beneath the breeze
adorning rock hewn shore and trees.

A Silence Of Green

The frayed green fabric of the patio swing
        dances in eight-six rhythm,
waltzing sporadically with the breeze.

An enraptured audience
of scattered pinecones
and rust-colored needles
sit in silent awe:

            Mesmerized,
        unable to applaud.

            Paralyzed
        by the strange magic
            of this rhythm.

        A worn broom
leans against a cobwebbed shed,
blindly staring at an overgrowth of tall weeds
        climbing the aged fence,
            entangled in ivy vines.

An orange tabby cat purring,
    and sparrows twittering
        are the only sounds
        breaking the silence.

Even the fluttering fabric
    of the patio swing
is too soft to be heard
        inside this deep,
            bold
        silence of green.

Against A Dry Sky

The fingers of rain flex
   against a dry sky of powder-pale-gray
     dimming the road I walk.
I retrace my steps
   searching for the footprints I lost
and the path that will lead me
      back to myself.

The sun has been gone so long
   and this hard rain is ever prevalent
     and relentless in its pursuit
   to wipe out all signposts and directions.

I am lost to the world and tossed
by a haphazard renegade wind
   into a lost moment in time.

I sit in the melting pot of my mind
   beside the ocean of my youth
     dropping burnt tears
     into the cold ebbing waves
   as the fingers of rain
     continue their flex
   against a dry sky
     of powder-pale-gray.

At The Lake

Upside down trees
and upright ducks
dance on the cake of life's waters
reflecting the real and surreal
on the ripples of icing.

Viewpoints are crossroads
into a world of dimensions
and contradictions.

   Conjecture abounds
in the lap of nature's realm.

Do the birds reflect
in a world of inanimate trees
or do the trees reflect
in a world of animated ducks?

Molecular structure,
atomic to subatomic,
   quark to muon,
   quack to rustle,
to reflection, to reality,
manifests continuously
in a surrealistic universe of interchangeable
upside down trees and upright ducks,
becoming a compendium
of possible impossibilities.

The ducks wade peacefully.
   The trees watch lazily.

I dimensionalize totally
     at the lake.

Atmospheres

I watch the water strider
      skating across the autumn lake;
          elegant, wistful,
      at home on its watery highway of dreams.

I see the mosquitoes
      bobbing and hovering
          over stale rain puddles;
              oblivious, unaware
      on ever-changing slices of air.

I hear the warblers
      chatting incessantly,
          trading comments and secrets,
      harmonizing the rustle of leaves
          in the dance of the branches.

We are earth striders
      walking across the sands of time,
          fingerprinting our footsteps
      onto the disappearing illusions of life.

Water striders, mosquitoes,
      warblers and earth striders;
          all sharing the same atmosphere
              in the catch
          of God's exhaled breath.

Autumn Colors

The world continues spinning around.
Seasons change without a sound
ushering in the colors of autumn.
A cool wind whispers of things to come:
Cobalt blue skies tinged with gray.
Nature's wizardry on display
ready for the race and chase
as autumn flees from winter's embrace.

The falling away of the leaves has begun.
They've outlived their season in the sun.
Bright colored leaves, gold, yellow and red
tucking summer's face into its bed.
Under a burnished sky of rust
the summer sun has turned to dust.

Tectonic seasons slipping and sliding,
the warm south wind's gone into hiding.
Raindrops bump and grind in the breeze
hypnotized by Fall's strip tease.
Nature quickens her pulse and pace.
Autumn burns out in a fiery blaze.
Leaves disappear without a trace.

The Robin's Broken Heart
(a sonnet)

Her feathers wet and ruffled by the storm,
upon a broken twig the robin perched.
The clouds, now ripped and torn, had lost their form.
She wept in sorrow perched on the leaves of birch.
Her red breast pounding from the pain within,
she viewed her nest in shambles on the ground:
Just broken eggshells where her hopes had been.
Her heart was breaking though it made no sound.
The atmosphere was heavy, musky, cloyed,
with desperation on this field of death.
The pale blue fragments of new life destroyed,
the birds of paradise have lost their breath.
The leaves have fallen down and turned to dust.
The red breast of the robin turned to rust.

A Hard Rain

A hard rain pelts down
graying the sky to charcoal.
The Quay is deserted,
and somehow out of key.

I stand at the guard rail,
collar pulled tight,
staring at the cold river.
The wind whirls and swirls
inviting the river into its frenzy.
The river resists, then slowly submits.
Small ripples at first
cresting to waves;
synchronicity somehow still present
in this simple chaos.

A young girl
in a pink fleece Parka
and well-worn mukluks
passes by,
her eyes as vague
as fading winter sparks.

The day dissolves.

Night chews on the last. remnants
of a non-descript twilight;
appetite sated,
she licks her lips
and the thunder rolls
in the bruised atmosphere
of a hard, hard rain
bleeding from the sky.

A Pale-Yellow Sky

A wayward star glistens
on the whetted lips of the breeze

Across a pale-yellow sky
a rising moon sits astride
the wind's coat tails,
riding slices of shadow
and shimmer,
spinning haphazardly

I, too, spin haphazardly
on a torn and tossed renegade wind
dissolving in the misty tears
of a dying sun
under the half-mast eyelids
of a pale-yellow sky.

The sky and I...
both of us
old beyond our years.

April Dew
(for Janet Kvamman)

April showers
bathe the soil to a sweet sizzle,
birthing the truest beauty
of purple, pink, red,
yellow, lavender and green blend;
dream dust come to life
in the seasonal earth.

Dew on the leaves
sun-kissed to vapour,
riding the wind,
to another morning.

Bursting through air.
Passing through clouds.
Becoming invisible fog.
Gliding through night
into the arms of dawn once again.

Tears on the leaves, stems and sepals
gently awake and quiver
shaking off the dream dust
and the disappearing dew.

April showers.
Purple flowers:
Sun-kissed.
Dew mist.

As I Lie Underneath And Deep Within

A sudden frost-bound wind
swirls softly
through ice-riddled fields of dearth;
and whistles
through the whispering pines,
as I lie underneath
and deep within.

The branches snap their fingers
in stony-faced repose
to the trance-like rhythm
of the atmosphere.

The bridge that overlooks the eddying stream
creaks to the drumbeat
of a thousand sighs.

I take no heed of brackish gathering clouds
that threaten high above my cold tombstone:
deaf to all the words you never said,
dead to all the deeds I left undone,
        as I lie underneath
            and deep within.

At Eventide

In the calm of the ocean at full tide,
there is a stillness
and silence.

In the deep of my pocket at eventide
there are smooth stones
longing to skip into
and over
the stillness of water
and the silence of breath.

Somewhere
there is a moon in full dress
and stars winking
at her shimmer
and
her shine.

In the palm of my heart, at rest,
there is a stillness
and a silence
nudged up against
the solid beating of my soul,

in the deep of my pocket
at eventide.

At Rest

At rest,
the boats bask lazily
in the gloss and shine of the bay.
Sparkling in the aftermath
and still fresh with the electricity of the wind,
the thrill of the ride whets the hull's tongue,

A residue of froth and spume
hidden at the waterline
slowly dissipates under dusk's silky caress.

In the hush of a grooved moment,
the boats whisper and chortle
through the thickening atmosphere
trading family secrets
on the slap and lap of the waves.

They gently rock in the bay's womb,
suspended in a timeless chasm
of motionless motion.
As fingers of darkness stretch
across the fast-dimming sky
palms open, gathering in
the last remnants of fading twilight;
fist readying itself
to close the ebony curtains of night.

At rest,
in the shadows of this small infinity,
the boats submit to the elements,
to sleep;
perchance to dream.

Beinn Eighe
(Ekphrastic poem written to the painting by Derek Young)

A diamond of great worth and depth,
alive with light and shadow,
lies beneath a layered sky
in silent majestic glory.

A spectacular, Scottish Highland path
climbs through the lush of a velvet forest
adorned with nature's magnificent pinewoods.

An archaic dimension of mood pervades
as the past moves through the present.

We walk through the sacred silence
of an ancient stone age dawn
that leads to the cap of Sgurr Ban;
the pristine white peak Beinn Eighe
that glistens with star dusted wishes
and whispers of what dreams may come.

Blessed Be The Rain

Blessed be the rain
that falls from the eyes in the sky.
There is a cleansing to this wet.
The fresh smell of soil and vegetation
escaping from the earth
infuse the atmosphere,
sweeten the air.

Raindrops bump and grind
falling in short lived expectation
crowning invisible dominions
holding court in nature's chambers
and disappearing mansions

Blessed be the rain
that falls from the eyes of the soul
filling the canyons of the mind,
overflowing the rivers of the heart
rinsing the spirit clean.

Blessed be the rain:
Keeper of raging rivers
and gentle streams.
The essence
of life and rebirth.

Burnaby Lake Sunset
(for Richard Klyne)

Sun melting on water
waning from hotter.
Tranquility abounds
far from city sounds.
A mirror of lake
shines in the sun's wake
promising soon
to reflect the moon.

Clouds pass by
high in the sky.
A lonely bird flies
on wings and sighs.
Flowers close petals
as twilight settles
on sentinel trees
touched by the breeze.

The sun will soon set
on this shimmering wet.

The moon will rise up
then dissolve in the dawn
and a deep sleeping morn
will awaken reborn.

Sunset ... at Burnaby Lake.
 Beauty ... simple beauty,
  just for beauty's sake.

Butterfly Effect

Dark and light wafer wings.
Contrasting pink petals.
Eyelids fluttering
within a sunbeam,
and beauty was born
formed into moments like this.
Cleansed by a raindrop.
Towelled dry in a zephyr.
Wandering lost
in this wonderland of colour.

Pulsating probiscis
sucking sweet nectar.
Feather light,
paper weight wings
caressing the petal,
gathering pollen,
scattering seed.

Slow motion,
kaleidoscope lens
zooming in
on this live Monet painting.
Bright dancing with dark;
magicians and angels
on vivid forest green canvas.

White angel wings.
Black magic hat.
Nature's wizardry creating:
          The beauty.
          The dynasty.
          The monarch.
      The butterfly effect.

Canary Universe

A speck of light.
A speck of bright.
An ocean of sky
          adrift on a rainbow boat
          sailing for lost horizons.

Not a raindrop.
Not a snowflake.
Not even a slow moving storm.
          Just a sun
that glares on our foreheads
   and renders, helpless,
      the exit of summer.

          Yellow streamers
          parade a celebrated sky
          too loud to go unnoticed
          or unappreciated.

   With silent applause
we acknowledge a canary universe
filled with specks of bright and song
as we glide our never-ending beach
                safe
in the comfort of each other's wings.

Canine Concert
(for Richard Klyne)

Early morning,
clean and quiet crisp.
Urban dawn breaking slowly
over a sleepy sunrise
Pale amber glow
pulsating in the mist.
Serenity broken
by coyotes in concert.
Cacaphony of howling
at the fading moon,
chasing it from the sky;
rabbit on the run.

This canine concert:
Always out of earshot.
Always just past the woods.
Never this close before.

Weeds of the wild
spreading onto our streets;
parading in packs
pushing the edges of forest
past the asphalt divider
into our concrete jungle.

4:30 a.m.
The cry of coyotes
on the lip of night;
a stir of echoes.

The incursion has begun.

Cat And Oranges

On the table,
a blue bowl askew, half filled with oranges,
the rest splayed out on the tabletop.
At the edge of the crime scene
the guilty cat peers over the table's edge
surveying the fruits of his labour.

He knows he can't put the oranges
        back into the bowl
and he knows he is going to be blamed.

He peers over the edge concentrating
on the bright colorful oranges.

Thoughts running through the cat's mind,
translated from feline to English,
probably involve the following:

> *'In for a penny, in for a pound.'*
> *'In for a dime, in for a dollar.'*
> *'Guilty by association.'*
> *'A cat amongst the pigeons.'*

After many minutes spent in deep contemplation
the cat jumps onto the table
and pounces amongst the oranges.

He bats them every which way
until they are all over the kitchen floor;
and then smiles inwardly with glee.

No sense crying over spilt oranges!

Cats And Jazz

The cat's in the cradle.
There's jazz in the cellar.
Blue notes purr softly
thickening the edge of emotion.

While the cat claws
its way into sleep's oblivion,
I dimensionalize
into the cellar sound;
the stellar sound.

I climb to the tip
of a raw red note
then slide down the edge
of a baby blue chord:
Upended.
Suspended.
Swaying to the riffs and groove
in the smooth of a satin heartbeat.

The cow jumps over the moon.
The dish runs away with the spoon.

  The music flows
  then slowly ebbs
into the sands of time.
  The revery dims;
      dissolves.

The cellar falls silent.
The cat in the cradle
    falls asleep.

The time for dreams is at hand.

Crab Boat

Sparse dreams peek through
a backlit navy-blue sky.
The dock in the bay,
now a dulled extension of the beach,
merges with infinity.

The waves lap gently at the shore,
a cat's tongue
caressing a bowl of milk.
Silk on sand, sand on silk.

In the distance,
the putt - putt - putt of a crab boat
invades the dreams of the deep,
echoing through sleeping pebbles
and submerged rocks,
through the skins of the fish
cracking dawn open
with haunting whispers;
slicing this early morning loneliness
w i d e open.

I stand at the edge of my mind
            recalling:
Shorelines and seashells.
Sandbars and castles.
A four-year-old girl standing
on a beach of dreams.

Aaahhh, memories...

They swim in my mind
with a bittersweet ease
on the ebbing waves
of a crab boat's fading
putt — putt — putt.

Crescent Beach Shoreline
(for Maryann Bowles)

The evening sky is crisp and clear.
With invisible hands
she props up a wet moon
more reticent than overt;
more hungry than thirsty.

The Crescent Beach shoreline is muted.
Tidal meanderings caress and rinse
the dark edges of seaweed and stone to a shine.

A bevy of twinkling stars
pokes holes in the black tapestry above
trying to save the sky
from being swallowed up
in night's gaping maw.

And all that dust and glitter
haloing the stars and moon
covers up their secrets, hides their poems
and blankets their silence.
But where does their silence go?
At what podium are their poems read?
At what altar are their secrets exposed?
The pages of their lives:
embers sparking, flickering,
burning out in the fading whispers
of days and nights that will not come again.
Where do their secrets and poems go?

The glint and glimmer of the Milky Way
lights our journey to the stars and back again.
From inception, birth, and breath
to exhalation, expiration and death
rising from cold ash to burning spirit,
the spark of soul never to be destroyed..

The evening sky is crisp and clear.
I am almost asleep in the arms of my familiar ghosts.
Drinking from the lip of the wet moon,
as it pushes and pulls at the Crescent Beach tide,
a dead memory enters my mind on soft satin slippers
that once trod the dreams of my lost yesterdays.

The wind whispers sweet nothings
to the tide as it slips away on little cat feet
into the burnt-out dust of a star
and the wayward sway of an evanescent moon.

The Crescent Beach shoreline falls asleep ...
        perchance to dream.

Crescent Beach, The Water, The Sun

I miss Crescent Beach, the water, the sun
and those yesterday moments time put on the run.

I never realized how fast time could fly.
In a fading parade days and evenings passed by.

There are treasured moments I'll always recall
that still warm my heart summer, spring, winter, fall:

Moments with my mother wading the shore.
I wish I could relive those moments once more.

But alas those yesterdays are long gone
and all that's left is their haunting song.

I miss Crescent Beach, the water, the sun
and all those sweet memories that have come undone.

Dance Of The Branches

The crows sway and prance
      on the dance of the branches.
            A blur of raindrops cloud the sky,
                spill onto the leaves,
           and dampen the moment in time
                to an invisible green ink stain
           on a pale grey canvas
      of passing thoughts.

I tap into the pulse of the universe
      and share its breath:
           to bring me closer to the crows,
           to understand the true rhythm
                locked inside the majesty
           of this magical dance of the branches.

I emerge
      from under the canopy of heaven
           into the damp tears of reality.

                I open my umbrella,
                a rounded scepter,
           to do battle with the army of raindrops
           relentlessly pursuing me down the lane.

I come to an intersection
                and stand there for an eternity
           listening for the dance of the branches
      to give me my location in time
that I may finally find my way home.

Dark Honey

A wet twilight drips dark honey
across the pale blue waters.

Darkness shawls across
the jagged shoreline I wander.

A bittersweet melody
riding the wind
whispers in my ear.

Once there were sunbursts
polishing the dull edge of days ...
days dragging their feet.

Once there was stardust
lighting up the dark nights ...
nights that seemed never-ending.

Like a beached boat
I wait patiently anticipating
the pale blue wash
of eternity's waters.

I stand beneath twilight's dark honey
waiting for a sunrise
I can hold in my heart

and a sunset
I can hold in my soul.

In The Garden Of Yellow Lanterns
(a tribute to Sharla's backyard garden)

Dusk falls casually
       in the garden of yellow lanterns
       surrounding the ivy clad tree.

There's a touch to the air I can almost feel
       in an atmosphere soft to the touch.

After the hot is burnt off the sun-streaked day
there's a breathlessness to the cool that invades:
       a smoky wish
       pressed through rose-kissed lips.

I place the warmth of my palm to my chest
       and feel the welcome melt and meld
          of the appendage to the shore
          like a ghost ship lost at sea
          finally coming to rest
       in its disappearing breath
as dusk fades
     to twilight,
       to night
          to dawn ...
     in the garden of yellow lanterns.

Deep Silver Silence Of Song

The darkness bites and cracks the snow and ice
     to wrinkle and slice the silence.
When the light falls on winter evenings
and the river makes no sound in its passing,
I watch and listen in reverence and awe.
Its reeds, frozen stiffer than glass,
are mute in this cold, cold silence ...
a silence that cannot be described or traversed.

At a moment like this, bathed in indigo and white,
     how can one anticipate the dawn?

But it does come, anticipated or not,
and slowly climbs over the tree-lined horizon.

     A blazing of sunlight
     thaws the frost-bitten
      land, sea and sky
into an evanescent kodak memory of July daze
and August haze and a promise to glaze the beach
    and shore with fresh sand and rain
for the coming of feather, shell, mica and quartz
as the higher ground cedar and shale
     whisper to the wind
  of days and nights to come.

At a moment like this, bathed in gold and turquoise,
how can one not recall hot, hot summer evenings too?

     The ice melts, the bite goes slack
      and the darkness abates
     in a deep silver silence of song.

Watering His Garden

The trees are mumbling today
and the grass is whispering secrets
to the flowers and the sky.

In the playground of my mind,
there are swings and see-saws,
water slides and monkey bars,
and on a good day ...
        laughing children all around.

Today is not a good day for play.
There are thunderclouds overhead
and the threat of rain and maybe lighting
     will soon be a reality.

        The trees know it.
        The grass feels it
    and the flowers and the sky
     converse with the rain
     in reverence and prayer.

God is watering his garden.

Horse Of Many Colors

Riding a horse of many colors
I accent the deep green of the valley
and soothe the landscape of my mind.

There is a familiar feel to the west edge of the wind
and an ancient knowingness drifting across the sky.

I give the horse his head and he leads me
into an emerald forest of forgetfulness
where all sins are scrubbed from the soul.

I spend many suns and moons in the hold
of perpetual, perfect days and nights.

On my last day, I cleanse in a waterfall
of absolution and forgiveness.

My horse of many colors returns for me.
I leave behind my teardrops
to water the deep green valley
and shine the emerald forest.

I ride my horse of many colors,
now a stallion of pristine white,
to where the angels reside
at the gates of heaven ...

      home at last.

West Coast Wind

I stand inside my silence.
      I can feel the atmosphere
      I can taste the salt air.

A small white dog
      strolls along the boardwalk
      intermittently barking
            at the seagulls crying overhead.

This is a west coast day
      and I am a west coast girl
      leisurely strolling beneath
            a warm west coast August sun.

I stand inside my silence
      savoring the taste of the salt air
      drifting lazily along
      on the coat tails
      of a smooth west coast
      tuxedo afternoon.

Butterflies And I

A flurry of butterflies adorned the sky.
Their colorful wings glistened
in the late afternoon sun.

 The damp of the dew
 long dissipated.

 Flowers and leaves at rest,
 relaxing.

I wind my way along the well trodden path
of left over footprints from absentee travelers.

Most of the birds have migrated
 to warmer climates.

The butterflies and I have remained behind,
 cocooning separately
 inside our winter dreams.

This October Night

Rain glazed street
streaked with traffic light flares:
green, amber, and red.

The silky glistening of these lights
somehow warms this cool October night,
and I am comfortable inside
its luxurious gleaming embrace.

I hold hands with the night
walking down paths of inglorious glory,
side-stepping the pitfalls of sin and folly.

   In the end
I come full circle back to myself
and look into life's reversible mirror
   and see myself
gazing at the rain glazed street,
 warmed in the cool embrace
   of this October night.

Ancient Gods

An image of a tattered scarecrow,
       and the fields
       in the fading light
       hazing out.

Sentinel cliffs,
       guarding
       an unfocused ocean
             that ebbs and flows
             at its leisure.

Ancient gods once lived here
beside this flowering meadow
that painted the face of these fields
a brighter shade of pale.

The scarecrow,
the fields,
the fading light
and the ancient gods
       lay sleeping and dreaming
             of past glories
             and better days.

In The Amber Glow

The pale fading sky
longs for old violin strings
and the brush of a dusty bow
to compose a melody
that burns a bluer shade of amber
in the burnished orange embers
that still flicker in the ether.

This visual, staining my soul,
vibrates with a stir of echoes
that travel the canyons of my mind
in search of old strings
to hang a song high.

High enough
to serenade the stars
and shine the amber glow
a bluer shade of gold.

Gloss Of My Mind

I step into the gloss of my mind
tripping down a beach of starfish gleam,
slipping through shallow sandbar pools.
I can see in the distance
a dark sky punctured with needles
   drawing black thread
   through the eyes of twilight
   sewing my wandering thoughts
     to the jagged edge
   of a shimmering evanescent moon.

The moon rests on a bank of indigo cloud
   dripping the last drops of summer
   from her tattered autumn dress
   onto the ebony blanket of night.

   My eyes grow weary.
   The beach and my wandering thoughts
     slowly dim, then fade
   as I step out of the gloss of my mind
   through the window *pains* of my heart
    back into reality's glare.

Dying Birds

I saw them overhead.
White doves flying in frantic formation,
hard against the wind,
chased by a posse of angry blackbirds.

There was no escape
They were marked for death.

They were tiring, slowing down;
easy prey for the hardy crows.

Clouds turned grey
against a fading horizon.
Fog fell over the mountains.
The doves crashed onto the rocks
and fell to their death
in a clatter of broken wings
and dead hearts.

In the wrong place
at the wrong time,
they were dying birds
          killed ...
by a murder of crows.

Ebony Stallions

Sweetening the hours,
the minutes flow like liquid honey,
pacing back and forth
inside their fleeing shadows.

The slick, ebony stallions
of the twelfth midnight moon
ascend with thundering hooves
on the horizon of equestrian dreams.

Their manes flow in prisms of light
through a river of translucent sky;
and their amethyst eyes sparkle
with the energy of a thousand stars.
They ring the moon in fevered paces
seeking heaven's coveted triple crown.

A hummingbird, with iridescent wings,
I flutter in motionless suspension
beneath a diamond studded chandelier,
          in the paling blue light
          of a slow spinning sky,
mesmerized by the ebony stallions
riding the rim of a ruby crowned song.

Sweetening the hours,
the minutes flow like liquid honey
as the ebony stallions fade from sight
on the horizon of equestrian dreams.

Echoes Of An Eagle
(a villanelle)

Against an opalescent purple sky
starlight flickering in the twilight glow
echoes of an eagle flying by.

High above the lovers as they lie
in flames inside the fire that burns below
against an opalescent purple sky.

And if they had wings, they would surely fly.
Amid this silence they have come to know
echoes of an eagle flying by.

Wrapped in the essence of a sacred sigh
Cupid softly sighs and rests his bow
against a purple opalescent sky.

Angels throng in murmurs and draw nigh.
Their wings of gossamer in stardust show
echoes of an eagle flying by.

Inside an antique pocket full of rye
a nursery rhyme resounds from long ago
against a purple opalescent sky
and echoes of an eagle flying by.

Eclipse

There was a moment
      that eclipsed the gray of day
and painted a splash of glitter and sequins
      across a nondescript twilight ocean.

And there was a pale-white, wooden schooner
drifting in the aimless crush of dreams I was dreaming
      at the close of that gray day.

And there was an evanescent moon
      rising high in a muted blue sky
          turning mauve
      turning navy
          to indigo inky dark.

And there was your ghost
          nuzzling my neck
      whispering in my ear
          floating and drifting
      across the universe divide of my mind
     in the total eclipse of my heart.

Eddying

In the core of the whirlpool,
eddying down,
flames of green and yellow
burn new pathways
for those who walk on coals;
those with scarred feet.

Under the pier
the water runs cold,
slapping and licking the pylons
with soft sadistic kisses.

On the surface,
air bubbles appear then dissolve
then appear again:
Punctured.
Reborn.
Punctured again.
Akin to the hearts of those who suffer.

> Under the skin
> rivers gone dry,
> passions burned out,
> flames to embers,
> to sparks,
> to ashes.

In the eye of the hurricane
wandering through the chaos:
Those with closed eyes.
Those with scarred souls
        eddying,
in the core of the whirlpool.

Disappearing Pools

Adrift on the mirror image
of one of my favourite memories
there is a pale violet sky sheen
backdropping the sunscape I am entering.

On this make-believe beach
I sit in my shady self and gaze in wonder
at the tanned bodies passing by
just outside the window I don't have
inside this house that crumbled like clay
into the sand I imagine I'm relaxing on.

I spy a cloudy rose agate
and mica, quartz and feldspar
from a fallen star.
lying beside a smooth, flat, shiny, black stone.

I pick up the cool black stone
and do a slow shuffle to the water's edge
of the ocean that isn't there.

In one slow, swift motion,
I skip the stone
and wonder about the worlds I just created
        in the expanding ripples
        of the disappearing pools.

Late Autumn In The Fall

The changing of the colors has come later this fall.
Mid November, and most of the trees
still have all their leaves.

The potpourri of colors is vivid
eye catching and mesmerizing.

The reds are so very, very red.
The yellows are overwhelmingly brilliant.
The burgundies, ambers and purples
accentuate the trees
like a radiant scarf
on an expensive Versace dress.

Late autumn in the fall,
a Panavision, Cinemascope movie,
delights the eye of the beholder
to the penultimate degree of perfection.

Late Fall Evening Rain

There is something about
late fall evening rain
that seems to shine the world
a glossier shade of wet.

Asphalt pavement
beneath a wet crescent moon
reflects the traffic light colors in streaks,
glistening matchstick runners
snaking under and around
the sloshing vehicles.

There is just something about
late fall evening rain
that polishes the world to a sleek satin shine,
       sparkling and beautiful
     in the caverns of my eyes,
imprinted onto the universal lens of time.

In The Sweet

Pieces of the past,
a heartbeat in the wind
and a bluff of cloud
anchored at the edge of the sea
on a horizon that seems to have slipped its lock.

An optical illusion –
both seem to drift
in semi-quasi unison
as if dancing to different songs
on two separate, yet overlapping,
sky auditoriums.

And then the sky darkens
and the tsunami of sound crashes
in thunderous claps and drum rolls
to announce the arrival of lightning
electrifying the stage below.

The heartbeat of the wind slows,
The clouds settle down
and sit back on their haunches;
and then the music plays
the sweetest sounds I've ever heard:

> A symphony in the sweet
> to soothe the weary soul.

In The Mist

Sitting in the car on the brow of the hill
        of Alberta Street
    the mist clings tenaciously
to the last remnants of the fading dark.

Late December
and a smattering of colorful Christmas lights
illuminate the misty street.

I see a girl with a dog
walking in the mist,
and I fancy I see Emily
walking down the sidewalk
with the dog she doesn't have.
The dog she'll never have;
and that makes me sad.

I close my eyes and sigh.
I imagine she is happy
in a parallel universe
walking through the morning mist
with the dog she loves;
a dog that loves her too
and makes her smile.

And that makes me smile
the sweetest of sweet, sweet smiles.

At The Quantum Level

Observe the spreading silence
as you stand inside the sound
        of your own silence.

The world passes by
in colors, scents, and music:
        Sometimes a lullaby.
        Sometimes an opera.

As these things pass by,
they pass through you.

Some leave a part of themselves
        with you.
Some are just visitors.

        BUT
    all impact you
at the quantum level.

A Ball Of Pearl Gloss

The night is cool.
      The moon is high.
           The air is full
                of knives and roses,
     and I am invading
         the dark of your heart.

Then the music starts:
     serenades, rhapsodies
         rock'n'roll, grunge.

The moon is a ball of pearl gloss
     adrift in the black water sky
         slicing the night with knives
     gleaned from the thorns
         of tainted white roses.

Caribou Country

In caribou country
the breeze blows a bit sweeter.

The birds in the trees
seem to whisper your name
and the forest knows you're there.

It's a Daniel Boone kind of feeling
when you're all alone
no one else around
and the rustle of leaves
is the only sound
as the fullness of the silence
surrounds you
in the warm hold
of Nature's embrace
deep in the heart
of caribou country.

Lone Orca

A lone Orca;
                black and white paint
          permeating blue canvas.

When the whale vanishes,
          the watermark
                    retains an invisible hue
that enraptures the seeking eye
                    and thrills the hungry heart.

Periwinkle Pond

The periwinkle pond sparkles
at the edge of the gathering flowers.

In the dark of the wood,
deep within the trees,
a song is being born.

A technicolour painting
splashed onto nature's canvas
begins to sway in the breeze.

A melancholy blue note
skates across the still of the pond
toward the distant city shore,
tuning the strings of streetlamp glow
to the music of approaching stars.

As twilight dims the face of day,
the periwinkle pond enters night's dream
then slowly falls asleep
inside night's lullaby.

Phantom Moon
(Ekphrastic poem written to the painting "Phantom Moon")

Midnight blue and twilight mauve
        gather the night into a lullaby
    above a sparkling turquoise stream;
           and all the while
      the phantom moon shimmers.

A gang of audience trees whisper and sway
    in the audio radiance
        of slick ravens crying soft overhead;
           and all the while
      the phantom moon glistens.

A haunting ambiance
    spills onto this moment of grace
          for a moment,
    for all time,
for almost no time at all;
           and all the while
      the phantom moon listens ...
        rapt in the spin
      of a star passing by.

The Seagull's Cry

A solitary seagull's cry
        stabs the lonely sky.

       Invisible blood spills
            from its surreal cicatrix.

       There's a living dream being drawn
       through the eye of heaven's dawn.

When the seagull disappears,
        the echo of its cry
            still stains the wounded sky.

The Spider

The wet spider's web
gleams in the aftermath of the rain
and the rays of an emerging sun.

A rainbow banners the intricate design
spun from the silver bark of birch dreams.

Inside this early morning stillness
the spider awakens
to spin new dreams in his web.

The day ebbs slowly.
The spider falls asleep
in the sleek black waters
of a midnight sigh.

Under the watchful eyes
of a billion twinkling stars
the spider spins another dream ...
deep in the dream
of a dream.

The Wishing Tree

*(Ekphrastic poem written to the painting "The Wishing Tree"
by Mimi Weiss and Candice James aka 'purple flame')*

Alone on the horizon,
attended to by birds,
the wishing tree is whispering
in poetry and words.

Against a tranquil sky
she stands in still repose
above a stand of trees
nestled down below.

The glowing purple rocks
whisper tales of glory
to anyone who'll listen
to their seasoned story.

And all the while the wishing tree,
whispering soft words,
relaxes in her quietude
attended to by birds.

There Comes A Magic Moment

Sometimes in the quiet repose,
before twilight enters
and ushers in the moon,
there comes a magic moment
from inspiration's child
awakening imagination
so, they can both run wild.

And, in these magic moments,
poetry is born and abounds.

Author Profile:

Candice James is a writer, poet, visual artist, musician, singer/songwriter, workshop facilitator and book reviewer. She completed her 2nd three-year term as Poet Laureate of The City of New Westminster, BC CANADA in June 2016 and was appointed Poet Laureate Emerita in November 2016. Her credentials are: Board Advisor to Royal City Literary Arts Society; Founder of: Poetry New Westminster; Poetry In The Park; Poetic Justice, Slam Central and Royal City Literary Arts Society; Past President of Royal City Literary Arts Society; the Federation of British Columbia Writers. She is a member of the League of Canadian Poets, she has been keynote speaker at "Word On The Street", "Black Dot Roots Cultural Collective", "Write On The Beach" and has judged the "Pat Lowther Memorial Award" and "Jessamy Stursberg Youth Poet Award". She received Pandora's Collective Vancouver Citizenship Award; and the Bernie Legge Artist/Cultural award.

Candice has authored 25 books of poetry with 7 different publishing houses: "A Split In The Water" (Fiddlehead 1979); was the first book published and the most recent book is "Spiritual Whispers" (Silver Bow Publishing 2023).

Candice has featured at many venues both civic and public and appeared on television and radio. She has presented workshops, mentored writers; written prefaces and reviews, published articles, and short stories. Her poetry has appeared in many international anthologies and her poems have been translated into Arabic, Italian, Bengali, Farsi and Chinese. Her artwork has appeared in Duende Magazine and in the "Spotlight" at Goddard College of Fine Arts, Vermont, USA and her poetry inside and artwork ("Unmasked") on the cover of Survision Magazine, Dublin, Ireland and her poetry and artwork have appeared in Wax Poetry Art Magazine Canada. Many of her paintings have been used as book covers for authors nationally and internationally.

Website   www.candicejames.com

Printed in the USA
CPSIA information can be obtained
at www.ICGtesting.com
JSHW060024120424
61032JS00009B/186